Though We
Are Apart,
Love Unites Us

Though We Are Apart, Love Unites Us

A collection of poems
Edited by Susan Polis Schutz

Blue Mountain Press ™

Boulder, Colorado

Library of Congress Number: 85-72418
ISBN: 0-88396-235-7

The following works have previously appeared in Blue Mountain Arts publications:

"I know that we are separated," by Susan Polis Schutz. Copyright © Continental Publications, 1975. "Today I woke up," and "I am always here," by Susan Polis Schutz. Copyright © Stephen Schutz and Susan Polis Schutz, 1982. "When you are not here," by Susan Polis Schutz. Copyright © Stephen Schutz and Susan Polis Schutz, 1984. "Our Time Apart," by Diane Hayes; "Today, I'm feeling the distance," by Lindsay Newman; "I missed you today," by Robert Stempkowski; "Every time I think of you," by Nita Daniels; "Missing you," by Dana M. Blystone; "Today, if a smile comes," by Paula Lee Carrico; and "I often think of you," by Tracy Thompson. Copyright © Blue Mountain Arts, Inc., 1984. "I Miss You," by Cathy Lynn Oaks; "You're on My Mind," and "Sometimes it isn't easy," by Collin McCarty; "Missing You," by Julie Anne Gridley; "I don't ever want to lose you . . . ," by Anna Edwards; "My Promise to You," by Beth Lynne Ellis; and "I have so many feelings," by Michael Niel Cameron. Copyright © Blue Mountain Arts, Inc., 1985. All rights reserved.

Thanks to the Blue Mountain Arts creative staff.

ACKNOWLEDGMENTS appear on page 62.

Manufactured in the United States of America
First printing: September, 1985

Blue Mountain Press INC.

P.O. Box 4549, Boulder, Colorado 80306

CONTENTS

I Miss You

*I sit here alone feeling so empty
  and lonely.
I think of you often —
every minute of the day,
wondering how you are,
  what you are doing,
    wishing I could hold you.*

*I sit remembering all we've shared,
  dreaming of all that will be,
and crying a tear for every minute
  we are apart.*

*At times I tell myself I am strong
and the time apart will go quickly,
    yet at others, I sit and cry
and wonder why love
        must hurt this way.*

*Though somewhere
        in the loneliness . . .
somewhere in the emptiness,
I find myself feeling very loved,
    and I realize that
it's not the loving that hurts so much . . .
    it's being without you.*

— Cathy Lynn Oaks

In our time apart,
you're on my mind more than ever . . .

I find that you're on my mind
more often than any other thought.
Sometimes I bring you there
    purposely . . . to console me
        or to warm me
            or just to make my day
                a little brighter.
But so often
you surprise me . . .
and find your own way
            into my thoughts.
There are times
when I awaken and realize
what a tender part of my dreams
            you have been.

And on into the day,
whenever a peaceful moment
seems to come my way
and my imagination is free to run,
   it takes me running into your arms
     and allows me to linger there . . .
knowing there's nothing I'd rather do.

I know that my thoughts are only
reflecting the loving hopes of my heart . . .
because whenever they wander,
  they always
    take me
      to you.

— Collin McCarty

Missing You

Sometimes when I'm
alone and missing you,
I remember the special times we've
  shared.
Sometimes the memories make me smile,
sometimes they make me cry.
Sometimes they make me lonely,
  but that's not so bad . . .
because remembering what we've already
  done makes me look forward
to the things we've yet to do.
It makes it easier to wait for you
because you don't seem so far away.
But more than anything else,
it makes me realize just how much
  I love you.

— Julie Anne Gridley

Our Time Apart

I *understand how difficult it is*
for you during this time of separation
because I, too, am suffering. I also
experience the loneliness at night
and the anger at life because of our
situation. I'm sorry for the times
I'm not there to share your happiness
or soothe your wounds. I'm sorry for
the times on the phone when I make
small talk, and all you need is a hug.
But there is one thing I'm not sorry
for, and that is loving you. Our
time apart is small when compared to
a lifetime of togetherness. If we
are strong, our love will not fade
with time. Rather, it will grow stronger
with each passing hour.

— *Diane Hayes*

Today,
I'm feeling the distance
*   between us*
a little more than most days . . .
I'm missing your smile,
*   your touch,*
*   your easy ways.*
I'm feeling a little lonelier
*   than usual,*
thinking of you a little more
and missing the way I feel
*   when I'm with you.*
Today, like every day that
*   you are away,*
I'm missing you
and wishing you were here . . .
Only today,
*   I find myself wishing*
*   just a little bit more.*

— Lindsay Newman

I missed you today;
We couldn't be together,
And I passed the time remembering
Happy yesterdays spent with you,
And anticipating many wonderful
    tomorrows.

I missed your smile;
That subtle yet unmistakable expression
    of your love
That melts away my doubts and fears
With its warm, unspoken reassurance,
And at the same time gives me a feeling
Of the happiness and security which only
Your deep and earnest love can give me.

I missed your touch;
The gentle caresses
*   that warm and soothe*
Like nothing else I know.

I missed your embrace;
The loving arms that hold me still
And let the love flow freely and silently
Between us.

I missed you today;
Because you are half of all I am,
And though I could live my life alone,
Life now for me is the constant sharing
Of our thoughts and feelings,
And the unselfish sharing
Of all our lives' experiences.

— Robert Stempkowski

We come together
for brief, beautiful
moments in time
And for awhile,
time stands still
And all we know is
the boundlessness
of our love

But then, as always,
time and the world
come crashing into
our universe
once again
And we must leave
each other

Yet, we are each
more alive
more nourished
more loved
than before
And we are both grateful

For we know that
we have a secret
treasure that only
a few may ever know

And we are content
in the knowledge that
we will continue
to grow, to share,
to dream, to love
together
in other beautiful
moments to come
           . . . in time

                    — Jane Caldwell

*When you are not here
I do everything I am supposed to do
trying to act normal and happy
when all of a sudden
I see something that reminds
me of you
and I sadly realize
how far away
you really are
For a few minutes I stop
everything I am doing and
I think about one of our
beautiful memories*

This brings a real
smile to my face
and helps me to
get through the day
But it sure would
be nicer
if you were here with
me
I miss you
so much

— *Susan Polis Schutz*

*E*very time I think of you,
I feel the sensation again . . .
   of loving you
and missing you like you
    could never imagine.
What I want more than anything
right now is to hold you
    in my arms
and tell you
   just how much I love you
and how much
   I want you in my life.

Please . . . don't ever doubt
my love for you . . .
because it is as real today
as it was
the day we first
began to share a love.

— Nita Daniels

When I'm Missing You . . .

The loneliest times are the times
  when I know I have nothing more to do,
Nothing left to distract my mind
  from thoughts of you.
The loneliest times are those when
  I have the day off,
And I know that you do, too,
  yet time and distance separate us.
Those are the worst days . . .
When I know I could be by your side,
  and I'm not.
The loneliest times are when I reach
  out for your hand,
And you're not there;
When I hear our song and I turn to
  read the love in your eyes,
And I see no one . . .

The loneliest times are all the times
  when I'm missing you.

— *Pamela J. Owens*

Without You . . .

I am trying to fill up my time —
take care of the emptiness I feel
    without you.
I am trying to remember that what
we have cannot be destroyed by
    distance.
We have made our communion with
    one another —
the bond that will not be severed.
I am trying to be strong —
    trying to cast out the doubts
    that distance brings.
If I could only hold you for a
    moment . . .
see your face, touch you,
then maybe I could be content again.
I never realized how much I have
    come to rely on your presence.

I love you.

— Sybie Hobbs

Sometimes when I think of you, I smile . . .
I smile at the good times we've shared;
I smile at the unforgettable times when
*   we grew close in our hearts and minds.*

Sometimes when I think of you, I cry . . .
I cry when I just want to hold your hand,
*   and it's not there;*
I cry when I think of how close we've
*   become, and how far apart we are.*

But mostly, when I think of you, I dream . . .
I dream of the day we'll be close again,
*   closer than we've ever imagined.*

*   You are constantly*
*   in my thoughts,*
*   in my heart,*
*   in my dreams.*

*   — Debbie Turner*

I wish that you were here with me
to watch the evening sun.
We could talk about the
day's events, both yours
and mine, and share
so many things.
And then with the satisfaction
of having tucked the day away,
we'd move into the nighttime,
with a dream or two, and wish
upon our favorite star.

I wish that you were here with me . . .
you'd be a happy ending
to my day.

— Jenny Sherman

When we are apart . . .

Sometimes it isn't easy
to be so in love with you . . .
to think about you
        all through the day,
to want to see you
        so much, to share
a knowing smile,
to want to whisper
    how special you are to me,
to want to hold you close
    and never let go.

Still . . . I think of you
    all through the day . . .
        so many nice things
            in so many wonderful ways.

— Collin McCarty

I miss you so very much and am constantly thinking of you all during the day.
Yet, somehow I feel that when this separation is over and we can look back on this time from a distance, within the warm security of our love, we will see it not so much as having kept us apart, but as having brought us closer together than we ever were. And we will appreciate more how much we have in having each other.

— Daniel Haughian

I thought of you today . . .
not once, or even twice,
but every few moments
it seemed the memory
of you came to mind.
I felt you today . . .
you are beside me always,
and not only beside me,
but inside me as well —
the image of you
is engraved upon my mind
and heart.
I never ask myself
if this is love —
I know it is.

I never wonder now
if I am complete —
I know I am.
You have made me whole
by your caring,
your understanding,
your love.
And in all my thoughts
of you today, I felt
the joy of our togetherness,
the security and warmth
of the knowledge of our love.

— Lin Oliver

Today I woke up
and thought about you
I went to work
and thought about you
I went to lunch
and thought about you
I went home at night
and thought about you
You are
always in my thoughts
and even though
*   we are not together*
you are a very important
part of my days

— Susan Polis Schutz

Missing you.
Loving you.
Thinking of you.
Day by day,
Hour by hour,
Minute by minute.
You are so far away, yet so near —
*   near to my heart,*
Sitting beside me in my memories.
The distance keeps us from
*   physically touching,*
Yet mentally, you have never
*   been closer,*
For the distance between us
Only makes my love for you
*   grow stronger.*

— Dana M. Blystone

I don't ever want to lose you . . .

*When you are away from me
I worry sometimes that something
will happen to you —
something that might take
you away from me
I know I should only have
good thoughts
but I guess I'm just a little
insecure
I can't help but worry
because you're the best thing
that ever happened in my life
You mean everything to me . . .
    and I don't ever want
        to lose you.*

— Anna Edwards

*For now
we are apart
and I miss you a great deal,
but I have not lost you
nor am I without you,
for your presence lives
in my soul
and dances in my mind
with each moment.*

My memories of you
are but smiles of my own,
waiting to be worn.
And though different dreams
might take us
to separate lands,
there are no forces
that can separate us.

Always
  we will be
  close in heart
  together in spirit
  and friends in love.

— Rowland R. Hoskins, Jr.

Loneliness

*Loneliness catches me at moments
when I least expect it.
I miss your loving arms around me.
I miss your smile so free and easy.
I miss your soul
     surrounding mine in complete love.*

*The time we spend apart
makes me more determined
to never take for granted
  the precious moments
    we are allowed to
        spend together.*

— Christine Lynn Moore

I wish we could be together
right now . . .

I *understand why we must be apart,*
and I know that in time we'll be
together.
I know I need to accept this as it is
and find some way to cope.
It's hard, and the truth is that
being without you hurts so much.
Maybe that's because I'm weak . . .
but I think it's because
you're wonderful.

— *Garry LaFollette*

My Promise to You

It seems the time we have together
is so limited
and it goes so fast.
I wish it could be longer,
but then I know that we both
have a long way to go
from where we are.

We can make no promises to each other
    because it hurts too much to break them,
    and the future is still unknown to us.
    And so instead we settle
        for simply sharing ourselves
            while we plan our separate lives
            together.
There is one thing, though,
    that I want you to know
        before time has a chance
        to pull us apart —
            a promise that will never
            be broken by my heart . . .

Even though we may become
    different people in different places
    and lose sight of each other
        in the future,
            still . . . the past cannot be erased,
            and there will be a part of me
            that will love you
                forever.

— Beth Lynne Ellis

You are away from me now,
  and I find my thoughts
constantly turning to you.
It is with happiness
that I recall
the many moments
we have shared together.

From the very beginning
I have known
that our relationship

was destined to be very special.
Kindness and caring
have always been
our greatest tools.
With these
we have formed
a love that has continued to grow
and that can survive the distance
that now lies between us.

— E. Lori Milton

*You and I are
in different worlds
tonight.*

*I wonder what you
are doing and if
you are thinking
of me.*

*I wish I could be
with you . . .*

to wipe out any
traces of the
lonely evening
ahead.

We could go for
a walk outside
and count the stars
in the sky.

I wish we could
just be together
tonight.

— *Ted D. Bidwell*

*I know that
we are separated
by many
days walking
but distance
can never
weaken our
relationship
For what
is in our
minds and hearts
is stronger
than any
outside force
And when we are
together again
our relationship
will be
that much more
intense and beautiful*

— Susan Polis Schutz

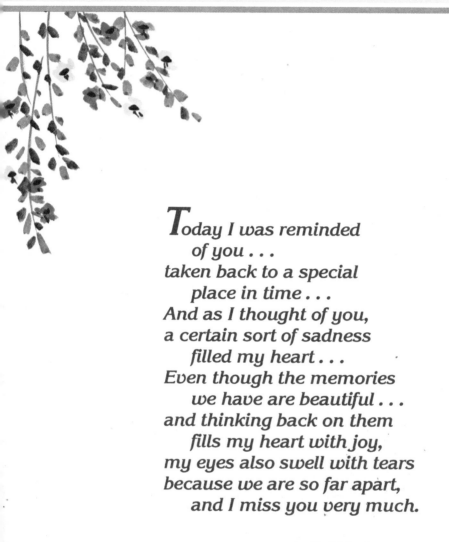

Today I was reminded
of you . . .
taken back to a special
place in time . . .
And as I thought of you,
a certain sort of sadness
filled my heart . . .
Even though the memories
we have are beautiful . . .
and thinking back on them
fills my heart with joy,
my eyes also swell with tears
because we are so far apart,
and I miss you very much.

— Debbie Avery

I haven't left you
I couldn't leave you
For how can our souls part
Time and distance cannot separate us
We can never stop communicating
Thoughts of love do not heed boundaries
Or time limits
They travel freely between us
And it is as if we are together
Close enough to touch
And, in time
In the right time
We will be together again
If it is meant to be.

— Rhoda-Katie Hannan

*Today I found myself thinking
    of you.
I thought of all that we have
shared in the short time we
    have known each other,
and suddenly I wanted to tell
you that you have left me with
    so many tender memories
to brighten my life when we
    are apart.*

— Teri Jackson

I am always here
to understand you
I am always here
to laugh with you
I am always here
to cry with you
I am always here
to talk to you
I am always here
to think with you
I am always here
to plan with you
Even though we
might not always
be together
please know that
I am always
here to
love
you

— Susan Polis Schutz

I'm beginning to feel
  the miles between us.
I really miss your company.
I miss the comfortable atmosphere
    you always seem to provide.
I miss the endless conversation
and the hours we spent together
      dreaming our dreams,
        setting our goals,
creating our lives
    and our futures . . .
for they were hours of strength,
  hours of friendship,
    and hours of love.

I will remember those hours forever,
and I will look forward
    to many more
      precious times
          with you.

— *Cheri Dale*

Loving thoughts of you
are forever on my mind . . .

Here I am again
sitting alone
daydreaming
*   about you . . .*
with dreams
that leave
a smile
in my heart.

— *Sheri Daugherty*

*Today, if a smile
  comes to you,
a happy smile
  that perhaps you
can't explain . . .*

*It's because
  in that moment,
I am thinking of you —
  and smiling, too!*

— *Paula Lee Carrico*

I often think of you in our distance apart.
I remember the times we've spent together
and the love we have.
These special times and our relationship
are the beautiful memories of my heart
    and my mind,
and I can openly and honestly say
that you are the most cherished in my heart.

I have grown to see lost loves
and to find disappointment —
I've seen hurt and sometimes pain,
and only now am I able to overlook the past
and see the goals I hope to reach.

I look into the future,
never really knowing what's there,
but wanting to see us together always.
We can only live to share our true feelings,
and to accomplish our hopes and dreams . . .
There will be time enough to see
if we can find our future together
and live for happiness,
forgetting those things in life
we would rather leave behind.

This separation is only a test of our future,
and when we know in our minds and hearts
that our feelings are stronger
than any outside pressures,
then when we're together once again
our relationship will be even more beautiful
than we've dreamed it in our times apart.

— Tracy Thompson

*Never a day goes by
    without my thinking of you —
of your touch
and your smile.*

And never a day goes by
without my wishing you
were here beside me,
sharing laughter
   and joy
      and the beauty of this day.

And never a day goes by
without my finding that
I love you a little more.

— Marsha Reid

I have so many feelings
and thoughts and needs
that I can find no words for . . .

I say I love you,
     but it is more than that.
I can tell you I miss you,
but that isn't nearly enough
to explain how empty
my heart, my arms, my life
get when we are apart.

I want nothing more
than to spend all my days with you,
and I look forward to the time
when we can always
     be together.

— Michael Niel Cameron

ACKNOWLEDGMENTS

We gratefully acknowledge the permission granted by the following authors to reprint their works.

Jane Caldwell for "We come together." Copyright ©Jane Caldwell, 1983. All rights reserved. Reprinted by permission.

Pamela J. Owens for "When I'm Missing You." Copyright © Pamela J. Owens, 1985. All rights reserved. Reprinted by permission.

Sybie Hobbs for "Without You. . . ." Copyright © Sybie Hobbs, 1985. All rights reserved. Reprinted by permission.

Debbie Turner for "When I think of you." Copyright © Debbie Turner, 1985. All rights reserved. Reprinted by permission.

Jenny Sherman for "I wish that you were here." Copyright © Jenny Sherman, 1985. All rights reserved. Reprinted by permission.

Daniel Haughian for "I miss you so very much." Copyright © Daniel Haughian, 1985. All rights reserved. Reprinted by permission.

Lin Oliver for "I thought of you today." Copyright © Lin Oliver, 1985. All rights reserved. Reprinted by permission.

Rowland R. Hoskins, Jr. for "For now we are apart." Copyright © Rowland R. Hoskins, Jr., 1985. All rights reserved. Reprinted by permission.

Garry LaFollette for "I wish we could be together." Copyright © Garry LaFollette, 1985. All rights reserved. Reprinted by permission.

Christine Lynn Moore for "Loneliness." Copyright © Christine Lynn Moore, 1984. All rights reserved. Reprinted by permission.

E. Lori Milton for "You are away from me now." Copyright © E. Lori Milton, 1982. All rights reserved. Reprinted by permission.

Ted D. Bidwell for "You and I are in different worlds." Copyright © Ted D. Bidwell, 1983. All rights reserved. Reprinted by permission.

Cheri Dale for "I'm beginning to feel." Copyright © Cheri Dale, 1985. All rights reserved. Reprinted by permission.

Debbie Avery for "Today I was reminded of you." Copyright © Debbie Avery, 1983. All rights reserved. Reprinted by permission.

Rhoda-Katie Hannan for "I haven't left you." Copyright © Rhoda-Katie Hannan, 1985. All rights reserved. Reprinted by permission.

Teri Jackson for "Today I found myself." Copyright © Teri Jackson, 1985. All rights reserved. Reprinted by permission.

Sheri Daugherty for "Here I am again." Copyright © Sheri Daugherty, 1984. All rights reserved. Reprinted by permission.

Marsha Reid for "Never a day goes by." Copyright © Marsha Reid, 1985. All rights reserved. Reprinted by permission.

A careful effort has been made to trace the ownership of poems used in this anthology in order to obtain permission to reprint copyrighted materials and to give proper credit to the copyright owners.

If any error or omission has occurred, it is completely inadvertent, and we would like to make corrections in future editions provided that written notification is made to the publisher: BLUE MOUNTAIN PRESS, INC., P.O. Box 4549, Boulder, Colorado 80306.